MAP
MY
STYLE

GW00692300

DOM & INK

MAP MY STYLE

Copyright © Dominic Evans, 2015

All rights reserved.

No part of this book may be reproduced by any means, nor transmitted, nor translated into a machine language, without the written permission of the publishers.

Dominic Evans has asserted his right to be identified as the author of this work in accordance with sections 77 and 78 of the Copyright, Designs and Patents Act 1988.

Condition of Sale
This book is sold subject to the condition that it shall not, by way of trade or otherwise, be lent, re-sold, hired out or otherwise circulated in any form of binding or cover other than that in which it is published and without a similar condition including this condition being imposed on the subsequent purchaser.

Huck & Pucker
Huck Towers
46 West Street
Chichester
West Sussex
PO19 1RP
UK

www.huckandpucker.com

Printed and bound in China

ISBN: 978-1-90986-509-9

Substantial discounts on bulk quantities of Huck & Pucker products are available to corporations, professional associations and other organisations. For details contact Nicky Douglas by telephone: +44 (0) 1243 756902, fax: +44 (0) 1243 786300 or email: huck@huckandpucker.com.

ABOUT THE AUTHOR

WORK IT SISTER!

DOM&INK (ALSO KNOWN AS DOMINIC EVANS) IS AN ILLUSTRATOR AND DINOSAUR LOVER LIVING IN MANCHESTER. HE LOVES TRASHY TV, SKINNY JEANS, HAWAIIAN SHIRTS AND COMICS.
HIS FIRST BOOK, MAP MY HEART, AN INTERACTIVE RELATIONSHIPS JOURNAL, IS AVAILABLE NOW!

WWW.MAP-MY-STYLE.COM

 @DOM_AND_INK

 @DOMANDINK

CONTENTS

SHOW ME YOUR STYLE

STYLE, INSPIRE AND SHARE YOUR OUTFITS WITH OTHERS! WHETHER IT'S YOUR NEW SHOES, HAIR OR A COLOURED-IN CREATION FROM THE BOOK... I WANNA SEE! LIKE, NOW.

TAG YOUR PHOTOS ON INSTAGRAM USING #MAPMYSTYLE

INTRO

NOW THIS BOOK MAY NOT COME WITH A FAIRY GODMOTHER BUT I'M JUST AS GOOD... WHY TAKE ADVICE FROM A GUY WHO HAS BIG HAIR, EXTREMELY (OUCH) TIGHT SKINNY JEANS AND A TASTE FOR FLORAL SHIRTS? BECAUSE I'VE SPENT 10 YEARS WORKING IN WOMEN'S FASHION, STYLING LADIES TO THE NINES! WALK INTO MY FITTING ROOM FEELING LIKE HAGRID AND YOU'LL LEAVE LIKE KATE MIDDLETON. WHILE I CAN'T GIVE YOU A BALLGOWN, I WILL GET YOU TO EMBRACE YOUR STYLE AND SHAPE, AND TEACH YOU HOW TO BITCHSLAP YOUR PRINCE CHARMING WHILE LOOKING DAMN FINE... I HAVE ONE RULE THOUGH, DO NOT BE PRECIOUS WITH THIS BOOK, I WANT IT RIPPED, COLOURED, SCRIBBLED AND STYLED TO DEATH.

SO CINDERELLA, ARE YOU READY TO GO TO THE BALL?

I HAVE A BIT OF A BEARD NOW. (IT'S RATHER SEXY)

ALL ABOUT YOU

I HOPE YOU'VE FLUNG THOSE
WARDROBE DOORS WIDE OPEN.
IT'S TIME FOR A SPRING CLEAN!

DRAW OR STICK IN A STUNNING PHOTO OF YOURSELF HERE:

SO. DAMN. SEXY.

INSPIRATION STATION

SO FIRST I WANT TO GET TO KNOW YOU. DON'T LOOK AT ME LIKE THAT, THIS WILL BE LIKE, SUPER FUN. I WANT TO KNOW WHAT DO YOU LOVE THAT INSPIRES YOU TO BE YOU? YOU CAN DRAW, COLOUR, LIST ON THESE PAGES... JUST DON'T BORE ME OKAY?!

TOP 3 TUNES TO TWERK TO:

1.

2.

3.

LIST THE BLOGGERS OR SITES YOU STALK/FOLLOW FOR FASHION TIPS:

FAVOURITE BOOK (NO TEEN VAMPIRES ALLOWED)

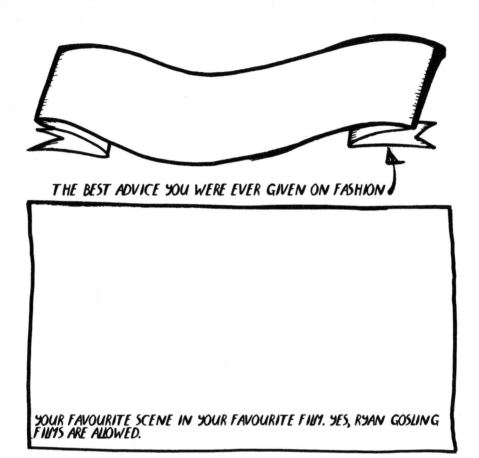

THE BEST ADVICE YOU WERE EVER GIVEN ON FASHION:

YOUR FAVOURITE SCENE IN YOUR FAVOURITE FILM. YES, RYAN GOSLING FILMS ARE ALLOWED.

AN ARTIST / PHOTOGRAPHER OR WRITER WHO MAKES YOU THINK DIFFERENTLY:

YOUR FAVOURITE COLOUR HERE:

UM. SO NOT ME THEN?

DRAW WHAT YOU LOOK LIKE ON A SATURDAY NIGHT:

↑ SKANKY-ASS
MIRROR
YOU NEVER
CLEAN

NOW DRAW WHAT YOU LOOK LIKE THE NEXT MORNING:

WOW. YOU LOOK LIKE SHIT.

SHE SAID WHAT?!

WRITE DOWN WHAT ALL YOUR FRIENDS SAY ABOUT YOUR CURRENT STYLE. THEY HAVE TO BE HONEST. I MEAN, DID THEY REALLY LIKE THOSE COWBOY BOOTS YOU BOUGHT LAST WEEK? NAH. DIDN'T THINK SO...

YOUR BEST FRIEND. YOUR SISTER FOR LIFE:

YOUR OTHER BEST FRIEND WHO YOU GET DRUNK WITH:

THAT CUTE OLD LADY YOU BEFRIENDED ON THE BUS HOME:

PRUNELLA FROM WORK. SHE DOESN'T LIKE YOU MUCH:

14

NOW THIS IS GOING TO BE HARD...
ASK YOUR MOTHER WHAT SHE THINKS
OF YOUR CURRENT STYLE. I MEAN, AT
LEAST SHE'LL BE HONEST RIGHT?

WHOA. SHE DON'T MINCE HER WORDS!

PIN-UP POWER

THESE ARE JUST A FEW OF THE BEAUTIFUL BODY SHAPES WOMEN HAVE. I WANT YOU TO GIVE THEM SOME COLOUR AND MAYBE A FEW TATTOOS TOO?

HOURGLASS

APPLE

BRICK

COLUMN

17

PEAR

PETITE

NOW DRAW YOUR OWN BEAUTIFUL BODY SHAPE IN THIS BIG OLD HEART!

YOUR BODY IS GORGEOUS. AND IF ANYONE HAS A PROBLEM WITH THAT I'LL KNOCK 'EM OUT!

LIST ALL THE THINGS YOU
LIKE ABOUT YOUR LOOKS,
AND ALL THE THINGS YOU
WOULD CHANGE...

KEEP   CHANGE

HOLD UP, THAT'S ENOUGH!
YOU'RE PERFECT THE WAY
YOU ARE!

DESCRIBE YOUR AWESOMENESS WITH ONE WORD...

STYLE CRUSH

IN EACH CIRCLE, DRAW OR WRITE THE CELEB WHOSE STYLE YOU'VE BEEN CRUSHIN' ON BAD:

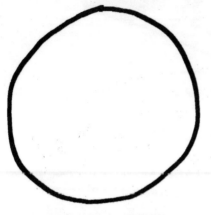

THE IT GIRL

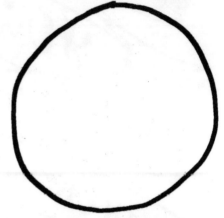

THE Z-LISTER

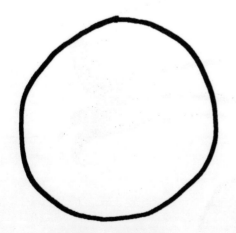

THE FIRST LADY

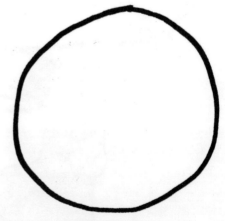

THE SUPERMODEL

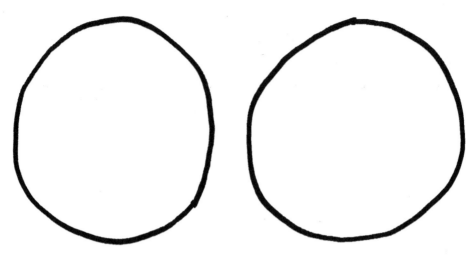

THE REAL HOUSEWIFE
OF BEVERLY HILLS

THE FASHION
BLOGGER

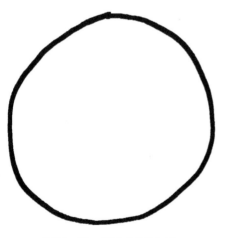

THE CLASSIC
MOVIE STAR

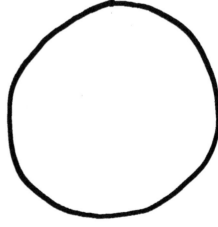

THE SINGER WHO
WEARS RAW MEAT

THE LIFE OF A TREND

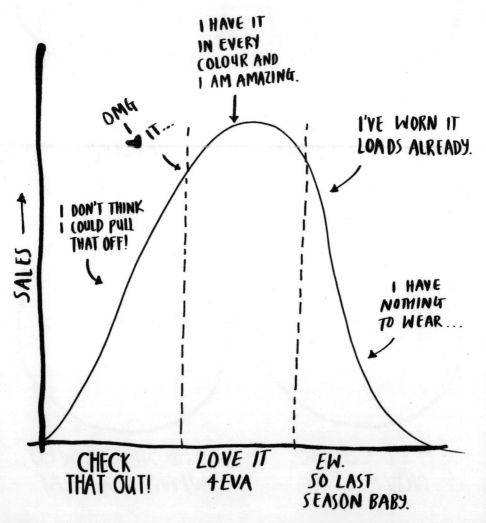

REMEMBER THAT FUR-LINED JUMPSUIT YOU BOUGHT LAST WEEK? CREATE A TREND GRAPH FOR IT AND ADD YOUR OWN LABELS:

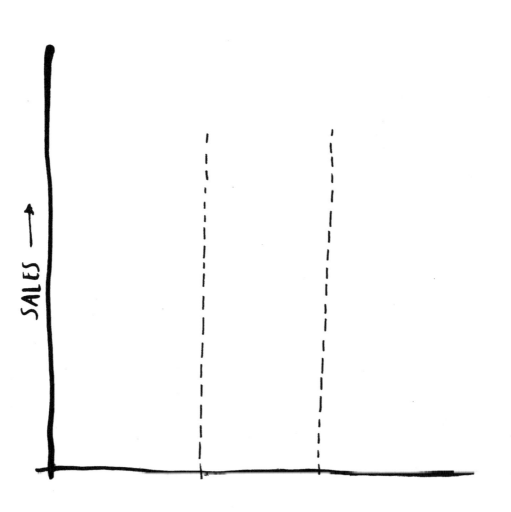

SALES →

DÉJÀ - VU

REMEMBER THAT NOVELTY JUMPER YOU USED
TO HATE WEARING EVERY CHRISTMAS?
THE AWFUL ONE THAT YOUR GRANDMA KNITTED?
REDRAW THE PATTERN FOR IT BELOW:

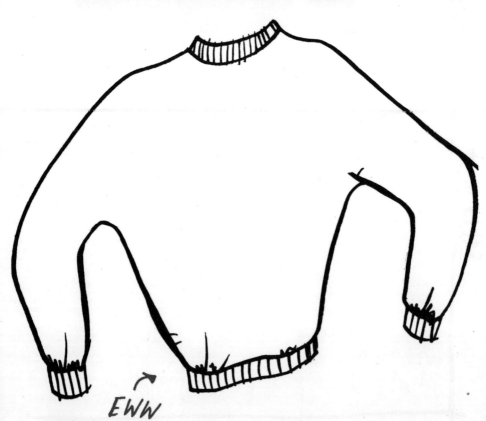

EWW

WELL WHADDYA KNOW, NOVELTY SEASONAL
JUMPERS ARE BACK IN TREND BABY! NOW
DRAW THE PATTERN OF THE NEW JUMPER
YOU BOUGHT WHICH LOOKS VERY SIMILAR TO
THE ONE THAT YOU HATED WHEN YOU WERE 12.
ADD SOME FESTIVE REINDEERS THOUGH.
I LIKE REINDEERS.

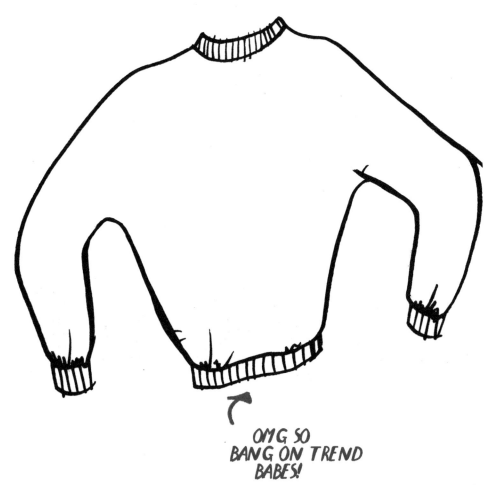

OMG SO
BANG ON TREND
BABES!

COLOUR ME IN

STYLE

LOOKIN'

IT'S ABOUT

AIN'T JUST ABOUT GOOD, FEELING GOOD TOO.

WRITE DOWN AN INSPIRATIONAL QUOTE. CUT IT OUT AND STICK ABOVE YOUR MIRROR. REPEAT TO SELF 5 TIMES A DAY. THEN REPEAT AGAIN AT 3 A.M. AFTER TOO MANY COCKTAILS AND A LOT OF KARAOKE.

CUT ME OUT!

SO LET'S TAKE A SELFIE

TAKE A SELFIE WITH YOUR BEST POUT. REMEMBER, THE HIGHER THE SHOT, THE BETTER THE CHEEKBONES!

TAG ON INSTAGRAM WITH #MAPMYSTYLE

COCO CHANEL

(18ᵀᴴ AUGUST 1883 – 10ᵀᴴ JANUARY 1971)

GABRIELLE BONHEUR CHANEL WAS THE FOUNDER OF THE CHANEL BRAND. SHE WAS KNOWN FOR DESIGNING CLOTHES THAT DIDN'T FOLLOW CORSET-SHAPED LINES. SHE ORIGINATED THE 'L.B.D.' AND THE CHANEL SUIT, AND HAS A SIGNATURE PERFUME. IT SMELLS QUITE NICE.

FASHION HAS TO DO WITH IDEAS, THE WAY WE LIVE, WHAT IS HAPPENING.

WORST

DRAW THE WORST HAIRSTYLE YOU HAVE EVER HAD ON THIS STUNNING SUPERMODEL:

UH OH, SHE AINT HAPPY!

BEST

DRAW THE BEST HAIRSTYLE YOU
HAVE EVER HAD ON THIS STUNNING
SUPERMODEL:

SHE'S LOOKING FOLLICALLY FABULOUS!

LO-BROW

I HATE TO TELL YOU THIS BUT YOUR
EYEBROWS NEED A GOOD PLUCKING.
ADD SOME MORE HAIR TO MAKE THESE
LOOK LIKE HUNGRY CATERPILLARS:

THOSE BROWS ARE BEASTLY!

HI-BROW

DRAW SOME DIFFERENT STYLES OF PLUCKED AND STYLED EYEBROWS THAT FRAME YOUR EYES AND SAY 'SEDUCE ME':

STYLE SWEEP

IF YOU DIDN'T HAVE A SHOPPING ADDICTION BEFORE, YOU DO NOW. WRITE IN EACH PRODUCT BOX WHICH STORE IS THE BEST FOR THAT PARTICULAR PRODUCT AND WHY. THOSE JEANS YOU BOUGHT THAT GAVE YOU KATE MOSS LEGS, WHERE DID YOU GET 'EM FROM AND HOW MUCH?!

DENIM:

BLING:

DRESSES:

WORKWEAR:

SUPPORT UNDERWEAR:

KNITWEAR:

HATS:

SHOES:

CHEAP-LOOKING
HAIR EXTENSIONS:

MARIE ANTOINETTE WAS ONCE THE QUEEN OF FRANCE.
SHE WAS KNOWN FOR HER ELABORATE, BEJEWELLED, HIGH
HAIR STYLE, KNOWN AS THE 'POUF'. COLOUR IN AND
CONTINUE THIS PATTERN OF THE FASHION ICON
AND HER CAKE. THEN AFTER, GO EAT SOME CAKE TOO.

THE WORK-IT WARDROBE

16 KEY PIECES FOR YOUR NEW STYLE THAT WILL MAKE YOU LOOK AWESOME...

1. THE WHITE TEE

NOT SURE WHAT TO WEAR WITH THOSE PRINTED SHORTS? HELLO WHITE TEE. OR WITH THAT TRIBAL MIDI SKIRT FOR THAT GIG? OH HELLO WHITE TEE AGAIN. THIS TEE WILL SAVE THE DAY IN ANY OUTFIT CRISIS. YOU CAN GET THEM OVERSIZED, ROLL-SLEEVED, FITTED AND CROPPED. BUY IT IN EVERY COLOUR, JUST NOT BEIGE. I DON'T LIKE BEIGE.

ROLL THEM SLEEVES UP

DRAW THE STATEMENT NECKLACE TO GO ON TOP OF YOUR OVERSIZED TEE.

2. THE STATEMENT JACKET

STATEMENT JACKETS ADD EDGE TO ANY OUTFIT.
MY PERSONAL CHOICE IS THE BIKER JACKET — TEAM
IT WITH JEANS AND A JUMPER OR A DRESS FOR A
NIGHT OUT. ADDED STYLE POINTS IF YOU POP THE
COLLAR AND SAY 'TELL ME ABOUT IT, STUD'.

YOUR STATEMENT JACKET DOESN'T HAVE TO BE A BIKER. IT COULD BE A BOYFRIEND BLAZER, A SEQUIN JACKET OR ANYTHING THAT MAKES A STATEMENT. AS LONG AS IT'S NOT A SEQUIN PONCHO. HELL NO.

DRAW OR LIST THE STATEMENT JACKETS YOU OWN OR WANT!

3. THE DAY DRESS

AN EASY DRESS YOU CAN WHACK OUT OF THE WARDROBE FOR GLAMOROUS OCCASIONS SUCH AS SHOPPING, MEETING THE PARTNER'S PARENTS OR FOR THAT TIME YOU BINGED ON DONUTS IN FRONT OF THE TV. DAMN, THOSE VANILLA SWIRLS WERE GOOD. SHIT, NOW I'M HUNGRY.

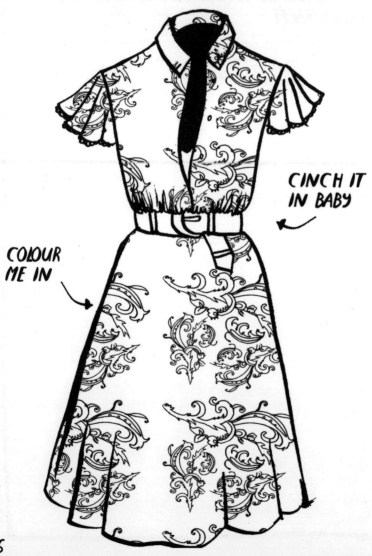

CINCH IT
IN BABY

COLOUR
ME IN

ADD A
PATTERN

HELLO FLIRTY
SPLIT

NOW LIST WHERE YOU WOULD
GO IN YOUR DAY DRESS:

AND DRAW THE DONUTS
YOU ATE:

NOM NOM

4. *THE JEANS*

FINDING YOUR PERFECT FIT IN DENIM JEANS IS LIKE
DATING. YOU GOTTA KEEP GOING TILL YOU FIND THE
ONE. JEANS CAN BE DRESSED UP WITH A TAILORED BLOUSE
AND STATEMENT JACKET (I WILL MAKE YOU BUY A BIKER)
OR DOWN WITH AN OVERSIZED TEE AND PUMPS. HAVE
YOU FOUND 'THE ONE' YET?

DRAW ALL THE STYLES OF JEAN YOU OWN:

DRAW YOUR DAMN FINE ASS IN THOSE JEANS...

OH, HEY BOOTY!

KNOW YOUR DENIM!

MAUREEN, THE CRAZY CAT LADY DOWNSTAIRS, WEARS JEANS COVERED IN HAIR, KETCHUP AND FINGERNAIL CLIPPINGS. DON'T LET THAT PUT YOU OFF EMBRACING A NEW FIT THOUGH! ALWAYS TRY ON. REPEAT THIS TO YOURSELF WHEN YOU NEXT FIND A PAIR. YOU'LL THANK ME FOR IT.

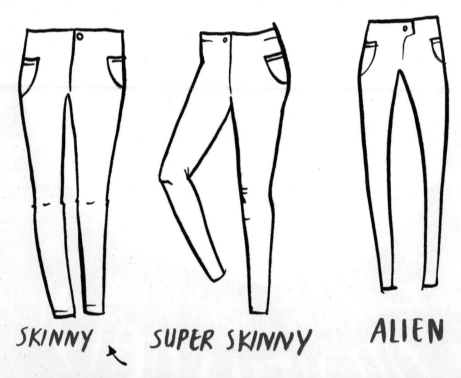

SKINNY   SUPER SKINNY   ALIEN

USE DIFFERENT SHADES OF BLUE TO COLOUR ALL THESE JEANS IN DIFFERENT WASHES!

STRAIGHT

BOOT-CUT

WIDE LEG

BOYFRIEND

← RIPS!

HIGH WAISTED
SKINNY

OUCH

MAUREEN

'Booty'
WRITTEN
HERE

Sexy girl

51

5. THE FLIRT SKIRT

SKIRTS COME IN ALL SHAPES, SIZES AND LENGTHS.
DEPENDING ON YOUR BODY SHAPE YOU NEED TO PICK
ACCORDINGLY. PENCILS ARE PERFECT FOR HOURGLASS
AND FULL SKIRTS ADD CURVES TO A BRICK. WHEN
YOU WEAR IT, BE CAREFUL, 'CAUSE A GOOD OLD SKIRT
CAN MAKE YOU FLIRT!

STICK IN A PHOTO OF YOUR LEGS AND THEN DRAW
YOUR PERFECT SKIRT OVER IT:

SO
LEGGY →

ADD SOME COLOUR AND PATTERN TO THESE:

FULL SKIRT

FLIPPY SKIRT

MINI SKIRT
(IN LEATHER?)

PENCIL SKIRT

MAXI

MIDI

A-LINE SKIRT

DIFFERENCE OF £5.00

6. THE L.B.D.

JUST LIKE MADONNA, THE L.B.D. NEVER AGES. REMEMBER, PICK A STYLE THAT ISN'T TOO TREND-FOCUSED, YOU DON'T WANT TO GET HUNG UP WHEN IT'S OUT OF SEASON DARLING!

THE LIZ HURLEY

ACTUAL XXL SAFETY PINS, HONEST

THE AUDREY

DRAW OR STICK IN A PIC OF YOUR L.B.D
AND ADD IT TO THE HALL OF LITTLE BLACK
DRESS FAME!

THE
ADELE

THE
BECKHAM

LENA DUNHAM
(MAY 13TH 1986 – PRESENT)

LENA IS A FILMMAKER AND STAR OF TV SHOW 'GIRLS'. SHE IS ALSO A WRITER AND PRODUCER. DUNHAM IS KNOWN FOR HER HUMOUR, QUICK WIT AND BOLD FASHION CHOICES. I'D LOVE TO HANG OUT WITH HER ONE DAY.

7. THE TAILORED DRESS

NOT TO BE CONFUSED WITH AN L.B.D., THE TAILORED DRESS IS ABOUT STRUCTURING AND SOPHISTICATION WITH A HINT OF 'MESS WITH ME AND I'LL BREAK YOUR JAW'. VICTORIA BECKHAM LOVES A TAILORED DRESS AND I'LL TELL YOU WHY; THEY'RE GREAT FOR WORK, ANY EVENT OR OCCASION AND MAKE YOUR BUM LOOK AMAZING.

← COLOUR THEM IN →

8· THE DENIM JACKET

THE DENIM JACKET PRETTY MUCH WORKS FOR NEARLY EVERY OCCASION. IT'S A SPRING/SUMMER WARDROBE STAPLE AND YOU CAN CRACK IT OUT FOR THAT GIG, DATE, FESTIVAL, SHOPPING TRIP OR ADVENTURE IN THE CONGO.

POP THE COLLAR FOR ADDED ATTITUDE! YEAH GIRL!

ROLL THE SLEEVES

LIST ALL THE OUTFITS YOU CAN TEAM YOUR DENIM JACKET WITH HERE:

9. THE PRETTY BLOUSE

THIS AIN'T JUST ANY BLOUSE – IT'S A POSH ONE! IT COMES IN A SOFT-WOVEN, SILKY-SMOOTH MATERIAL WITH A BOLD PRINT OR COLOUR ALL OVER IT. YOU CAN WEAR IT WITH JEANS FOR DAYTIME CLASS OR WITH A TAILORED SKIRT FOR THAT INTERVIEW TO BE THE NEXT TOP MODEL – WORK IT, BABY!

ADD SOME COLOUR AND A PRINT TO THIS

10. THE STATEMENT DRESS

IT'S THAT MOMENT YOU WALK INTO THE BAR, ALL EYES ARE ON YOU AND YOU'RE LIKE 'BOW DOWN MERE MORTALS TO MY SHIT-HOT STATEMENT DRESS Y'ALL!'. YOU HAVE SO MANY OPTIONS HERE; ONE-SHOULDER, SHORT, LONG, BACKLESS AND OF COURSE SEQUINS. IT'S A STATEMENT DRESS, IT NEEDS SOMETHING SHINY!

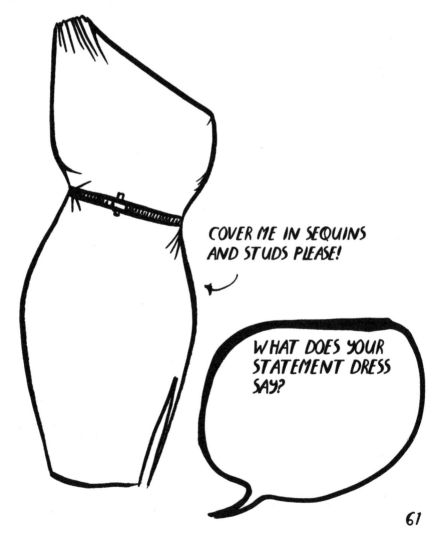

COVER ME IN SEQUINS AND STUDS PLEASE!

WHAT DOES YOUR STATEMENT DRESS SAY?

11. THE ALL-IN-ONE

JUMPSUITS AND PLAYSUITS ARE HERE TO STAY SO GET
OVER IT! NEED AN ALTERNATIVE TO THE L.B.D. OR THE
STATEMENT DRESS? THEN GET THAT ALL-IN-ONE ON.
DESIGN YOUR OWN ALL-IN-ONE, CONSIDERING BODY SHAPE,
STYLE, BOLD PATTERN AND HOW QUICKLY YOU CAN GET
IT OFF TO USE THE TOILET...

COLLAR ↪

LEG
LENGTH
↓

12. THE CARDIGAN

A GOOD CARDI CAN DO A GIRL GOOD. LIKE A DENIM JACKET THEY GO WITH EVERYTHING AND ARE PERFECT FOR A SMART/CASUAL OUTFIT (SMASUAL, BABY). ALSO THEY ARE FIERCE HIDERS AND PROTECTORS OF DODGY UNDER ARMS AND HORRIFIC TAN LINES.

PRINTED CARDIS WORK WELL TOO:

ADD A PATTERN

COLOUR THIS IN

13. THE SEXY TROUSERS

FOR DAYS WHEN DENIM WON'T CUT IT, SMART TROUSERS ARE AN I.O.U. (INSTANT OUTFIT UPGRADE). HOWEVER, YOU NEED TO PICK THE RIGHT STYLE FOR YOUR SHAPE AND ALWAYS TRY IT ON. I'VE FOUND THAT TAPERED CHINOS ARE A SAFE OPTION. COLOUR IN THIS PIC, RIP IT OUT AND TAKE TO YOUR NEAREST WOMENSWEAR RETAILER!

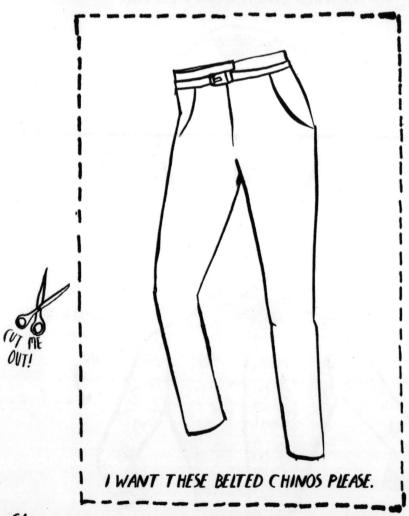

CUT ME OUT!

I WANT THESE BELTED CHINOS PLEASE.

HERE ARE SOME MORE STYLES:

WIDE LEG

PEG LEG

CAPRI

TAPERED

OTHER SEXY TROUSER STYLES I KNOW:

14. THE MAXI DRESS

MAXI DRESSES CAN BE SMART OR CASUAL AND EASILY DRESSED EITHER WAY. ANOTHER GOOD POINT IS THAT YOU DON'T NEED TO SHAVE THEM LEGS ...

ADD PRINT AND COLOUR TO MAKE THESE POP!

15. THE VEST TOP

ADD A PRINT
OR PATTERN TO
THIS BAD BOY!

PERFECT TO GO UNDER A BRIGHT JACKET OR TEAMED
WITH A CHEEKY PAIR OF PRINTED TROUSERS. YOU CAN
GET JERSEY VESTS FOR A CASUAL LOOK OR SILKY-SMOOTH
ONES TO ADD SOME OUTFIT FLAVOUR. SOD IT, BUY TWO.

16. THE WHITE SHIRT

JUST A PLAIN WHITE SHIRT I HEAR YOU SAY?
OH HELL YEAH. ONE WITH A FIERCE COLLAR AND
A CRISP CUT BECAUSE THIS SHIRT GOES ON
TOP OF, UNDER, TUCKED INTO AND WITH
EVERYTHING!

DRAW THE CUTE JUMPER IT GOES UNDER:

UNDER A DRESS OR MAYBE A PINAFORE? DRAW IT ON TOP!

LIST WHAT ELSE YOUR WHITE SHIRT CAN TEAM UP WITH:

-
-
-
-
-
- WITH A PLEATED SKIRT AND PIGTAILS. HELLO BRITNEY

SHOW ME WHAT THE COFFEE STAIN YOU GET ON YOUR SHIRT AFTER WEARING IT FOR JUST FIVE MINUTES LOOKS LIKE:

CAREFUL! ↗

DRAW/LIST ALL YOUR DIFFERENT CAPSULE OUTFITS:

OI! I TOLD YOU TO BURN THAT GREEN
LEOTARD! YOU REALLY WANT IT? WELL
GO JOIN THE X-MEN THEN.

LIST ON ONE SIDE ALL THE CLOTHES YOU WANT FOR YOUR WARDROBE AND THEN LIST ALL THE CLOTHES YOU NEED. FACE IT LOVE, PAYDAY IS LIKE A MONTH AWAY AND YOU DO NEED SOME NEW SPANX.

WANT

- A PENCIL SKIRT THAT MAKES ME LOOK LIKE I HAVE A KARDASHIAN BUM

NEED

- NEW BRIDGET JONES UNDERWEAR

- NEW <u>SEXY</u> UNDERWEAR

- TO MOVE OUT OF MY MUM'S

OI! KEEP IT TO FASHION...

WRITE YOUR OWN INSPIRATIONAL FASHION MANTRA ON THIS SCROLL:

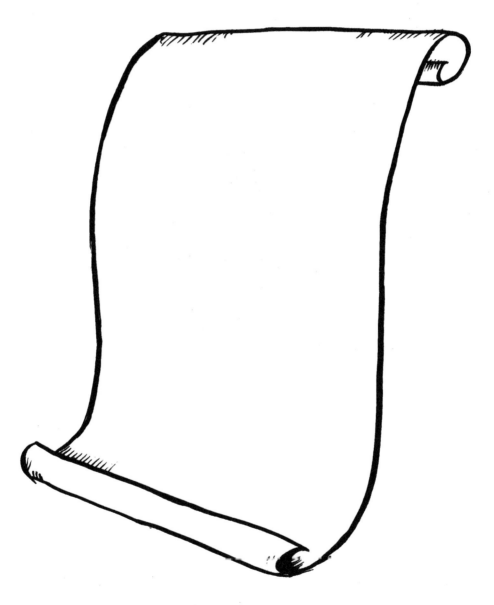

I HEAR YA SISTER!

IN ONE WORD WHO ARE YOU GOING TO BE TODAY?

HOW TO CHARITY SHOP

DON'T PULL THAT FACE AT ME. CHARITY SHOPS ARE A HIDDEN GOLDMINE OF FASHION GEMS. TRUST ME, ONCE YOU FIND THAT SEQUIN JACKET THAT'S CHEAPER THAN YOUR BUS FARE YOU WON'T STOP BANGING ON ABOUT 'EM.

1 ALWAYS HAVE A LIST. MAKE IT HERE:

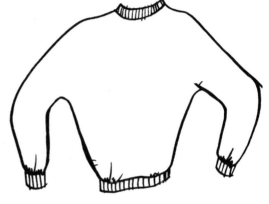

2 DONATE YOUR OLD STUFF. WHY NOT? IF YOU AIN'T GONNA BE WEARIN', THEN GET SHARIN'! COLOUR IN THE JUMPER YOU'RE GIVING BACK

3 ALWAYS TRY ON AND ALWAYS WASH THEM ONCE BOUGHT. NOW DRAW OR LIST ALL THE CHARITY SHOP SWAG YOU GOT TODAY:

FASHIONS FADE

STYLE IS ETERNAL

♥ YVES SAINT LAURENT ♥

WHICH FASHION THEME ARE YOU?

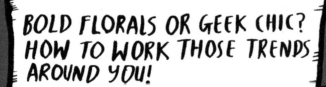

BOLD FLORALS OR GEEK CHIC?
HOW TO WORK THOSE TRENDS
AROUND YOU!

WILD ANIMAL

WHEN STYLED RIGHT, ANIMAL PRINT CAN TICK A LOT OF FASHION BOXES. GET IT WRONG AND RISK LOOKING LIKE SHERE KHAN ON ACID. MOVE OVER TARZAN, THE QUEEN OF THE JUNGLE HAS ARRIVED! ARE YOU READY TO ROAR?

SPICE UP OLD JEANS WITH A CLASSIC PRINTED JUMPER

LIST THE ANIMAL PRINT PIECES YOU OWN:

COLOUR THIS
BOXY-FIT SHIRT

TOP KNOTS
ROCK

ADD A
HANDBAG

ADD A
CLUTCH

COLOUR
THIS
PRINT

FOR A
STRIKING
SILHOUETTE
ADD TIGHTS

DAY   NIGHT

FLIRTY FLORALS

ALL-YEAR-ROUND FLORALS ARE ON TREND, WHETHER IT BE PASTEL-COLOURED SUMMER FLORALS OR DARK WINTER-STYLED FLORALS. YOU CAN NEVER GO WRONG WITH THESE:

THE SHIFT DRESS!

DRAW THE PERFECT TOP TO GO WITH THE SKIRT:

FLORALTASTIC SCARF

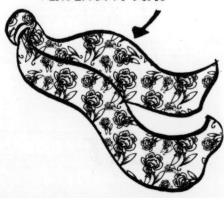

QUEEN OF ROCK

WHILE NOT DIRECTLY INFLUENCED BY ROCK, THIS ALTERNATIVE LOOK IS ABOUT CHANNELLING YOUR INNER COURTNEY LOVE AND KATE MOSS WITH TOUCHES OF LEATHER, FRINGING, SEQUINS AND STATEMENT EVERYTHING. THE HAIR IS LONG, THE LEGS LETHAL AND THE MAKE-UP DEADLY. IN THE SUMMER MONTHS YOUR FESTIVAL WARDROBE IS NAILED AND COME WINTER, UPDATE WITH LEATHER SKIRTS AND TROUSERS. YEAH, BABY!

ADD SOME KILLER EYE SHADOW AND SOME BROWS:

DRAW SOME SEQUINS ON TOP OF THIS OVERSIZED CROP TOP. LIKE SO TRENDY.

USE TWO COLOURS TO GIVE HER SOME TWO-TONE HAIR!

DAY   NIGHT

CLEAN CUT

CLASSIC TAILORING WITH A CONTEMPORARY TWIST.
THINK BETTY DRAPER MEETS MICHELLE OBAMA WITH
FULL SKIRTS, PLEATED SHIRTS, PASTEL COLOURS AND
PIPED FULL MACS. THIS IS IDEAL FOR TAKING YOU
FROM THE OFFICE TO THE COCKTAIL BAR. AND THE
BAR AFTER THAT... AND THE BAR AFTER THAT TOO.

MAC FOR ALL SEASONS

DRAW ME THE BLOUSE TO
GO WITH THESE SHORTS:

TAILORED PASTEL SHORTS.
COLOUR 'EM IN:

85

GEEK CHIC

A GOOD PAIR OF GLASSES WILL GET YOU EVERYWHERE THESE DAYS. GEEK CHIC IS SIMPLE, NOT TOO FUSSY BUT STILL ON TREND. OUTFIT BUILD WITH DENIM SHORTS AND SKIRTS, DAY DRESSES, KNITWEAR AND OF COURSE, A STAR WARS TEE. YOU'RE MY KINDA GIRL!

DRAW SOME GEEK GLASSES

DISTRESS THESE SHORTS

DRAW THE COMIC COVERS FOR YOUR COLLECTION!

DAY

NIGHT

RACEY LACY

LACE CAN DRESS UP ANY OUTFIT INSTANTLY. PASTEL LACE IS ALWAYS ON TREND FOR SPRING/SUMMER AND THEN MOVING INTO WINTER THE DARK NAVY, CREAM AND BLACK COMES INTO PLAY. THOUGH BE CAREFUL WHEN WEARING — ONE MISPLACED HOLE IN THAT OVERSIZED SHIRT AND THAT IS A NIPPLE FLASH WAITING TO HAPPEN.

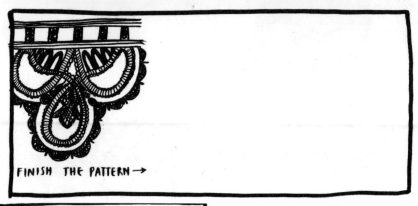

FINISH THE PATTERN →

DRAW THE HOLE IN THE DRESS YOU GOT AFTER YOU TRIPPED ON THE NIGHT BUS:

HELLO OVERSIZED LACE SHIRT. COLOUR IT IN:

WHICH FASHIONISTA DO YOU KNOW?

TICK THE BOXES ON WHICH FASHIONISTA YOU'VE MET OR TACKLED TO THE GROUND IN A SAMPLE SALE OVER THOSE LOUBOUTINS.

THE STYLE LOYALIST ☐

I BELIEVE IN CLASSIC STYLE. I'LL KEEP PIECES FOR YEARS AND WEAR THEM AGAIN AND AGAIN AND AGAIN AND AGAIN AND AGAIN. I LOVE THE COLOUR BLACK AND A GOOD ROLL-NECK.

THE BLENDER-INNER ☐

I DON'T LIKE TO WEAR ANYTHING TOO FASHIONY. CRAZY FASHION FOR ME IS A PINK T-SHIRT AND TROUSERS. WHOA. EVEN THAT JUST BLEW MY BRAIN. I LIKE TO BLEND IN SO I CAN LINGER IN SHOPS AND STARE AT PEOPLE.

THE FASHION ROAD KILLER ☐

I'LL TAKE THREE TRENDS AND WEAR THEM AT ONCE! MY FRIENDS SAY I'M LIKE, REALLY 'FUNKY'! OH, IS THAT A NEW FLORAL HEADBAND I CAN WEAR WITH MY LEOPARD PRINT HAREM PANTS AND POLKA DOT SHOES?!

THE DARLING ☐

OH MWAH MWAH (INSERT AIR KISSES) DARLING, DON'T YOU LOVE MY NEW VALENTINO DRESS. I KNOW DARLING JUST A LITTLE SOMETHING I PICKED UP YAHHH. GOT TO RUN AND SCHMOOZE DARLING, MWAH MWAH LOVE YOU DARLING LOVE YOU.

THE BULK BUYER ☐

I HAVE THIS PARTY NEXT TUESDAY SO I ORDERED 10 DRESSES ONLINE AND I'VE BOUGHT 20 MORE TODAY IN STORE. BUT I STILL DON'T HAVE ANYTHING TO WEAR! I'LL JUST WEAR THAT OLD DRESS THAT I BOUGHT LAST WEEK THEN...

THE VINTAGER ☐

THERE'S VINTAGE AND THEN THERE'S EXTREME VINTAGE LIKE ME! IF IT'S GOT SHOULDER PADS, FRILLS, VELVET, WIDE LEGS AND MAKES ME LOOK LIKE I'M ON BOARD THE YELLOW SUBMARINE ALL DAY LONG THEN I'LL TAKE IT, LOVE!

THE BARGAINER ☐

IT WAS 90 THEN 50, NOW, GUESS HOW MUCH I GOT IT FOR?! GO ON GUESS! GUESS!!!! YEP, GOT IT FOR 10. HOW GOOD IS THAT? WILL I WEAR IT? PROBABLY NOT.

THE TRENDER ☐

SO YEAH, LIKE, I'LL WEAR SOMETHING AND THEN I'LL PUT IT ONTO TWITTER AND THEN EVERYONE'S LIKE 'OH MY GOD YOU LOOK SO GOOD' AND I'M LIKE 'I KNOW'. SOMETIMES I THINK I'M TOO AHEAD OF THE TRENDS. MY FACEBOOK PAGE IS ALL PICTURES OF ME POSING BY BRICK WALLS AND CANALS LOOKING LIKE REALLY TRENDY. I'M KIND OF A BIG DEAL.

DRAW HER

STYLE SCENARIOS

THAT JOB INTERVIEW YOU HAVE ON MONDAY? NO PROBLEMO, I GOT IT COVERED...

COVER GIRL

GLAM
woman ♥

YOU'VE MADE IT ONTO THE COVER OF YOUR
MUM'S FAVOURITE MAGAZINE! NEXT STOP, VOGUE.
DRAW YOURSELF ON THE COVER LOOKING ALL GOOD.

JUST CHILLIN'

REMEMBER THAT SHIRT YOUR EX-BOYFRIEND LEFT YEARS AGO THAT YOU'VE BEEN USING AS A FLOOR CLOTH? WELL LET'S TURN IT FROM STAIN SCRUBBER TO WARDROBE STAPLE.

BELT IT

DON'T FEEL YOU CAN PULL OFF THE OVERSIZED LOOK? THEN JUST CINCH THAT SHIRT RIGHT IN WITH A BELT. TEAM WITH SKINNY JEANS AND BOOM: YOU LOOK AWESOME.

BUTTON IT

CHANNEL YOUR INNER PREPPY AND BUTTON THAT BAD BOY RIGHT UP. YEP, TO THE TOP. DRAW A STATEMENT NECKLACE ON TOP FOR ADDED STYLE CRED.

OPEN IT

WEAR UNBUTTONED OVER A JERSEY DRESS OR STYLE WITH A SIMPLE VEST TOP AND JEANS. ADD SOME GEEK GLASSES AND GO ALL LIKE, TOTALLY, HIPSTER.

SLASH IT

WHO NEEDS SLEEVES ANYWAY? CUT THE ARMS OFF AND WEAR OPEN OVER A VEST OR TIE AT THE WAIST IF FEELING DARING. GO ON BE A REBEL

COLOUR US IN!

LIST WHAT ELSE YOU COULD DO WITH YOUR SHIRT:

NOW TAKE A PIC AND TAG IT ON INSTAGRAM WITH #MAP MYSTYLE!

THRIFT SALE CHIC

YOU'VE GOT UP AT 6 A.M. FOR THIS THRIFT SALE DOWN THE ROAD. THINK OF ALL THE FASHION BARGAINS YOU CAN FIND THERE. AND THERE'S A FREE HOT DOG STAND. GET. THERE. NOW! ON THESE PAGES PUT TOGETHER YOUR LOOK AND YOUR DAY:

ADD A PATTERN TO THIS CAMI:

YOU'RE GONNA NEED A BIG SHOPPING BAG FOR ALL THOSE BARGAINS. DRAW IT:

DRAW YOUR HAIRSTYLE HERE:

DO THE MAKE-UP. GIVE ME SOME CASUAL SMOULDERING REALNESS:

ADD COLOUR TO THIS
COLOURED DENIM JACKET:

DRAW THE *AWKWARD* YET
ATTRACTIVE THRIFT SHOP
OWNER:

LIST ALL THE THINGS
YOU BOUGHT:

LET'S GET SMASUAL

IT'S SIMPLE. SMART AND CASUAL EQUALS SMASUAL. JUST TAKE
SOME SIMPLE CASUAL DAYWEAR THEN SMARTEN IT RIGHT
UP WITH A KEY PIECE FROM YOUR WARDROBE FOR ADDED
SMASUAL EFFECT. SHOES, JACKETS AND JEWELLERY ARE
INSTANT SMASUAL UPGRADES F.Y.I.

LIST THE PLACES
YOU'D GO SMASUAL:

· EXHIBITIONS
· DATES
· THE TAKEAWAY
·
·
·
·

SHOES OR BOOTS?

YOU NEED A STATEMENT JACKET
FOR THIS LOOK. DRAW THE REST
OF THE OUTFIT (AND YOU):

THE HIPSTERS IN THE GOURMET
COFFEE SHOP CAN SEE YOU FROM
THEIR WINDOW. DRAW YOURSELF
LOOKING DAMN SMASUAL WALKING
PAST WITH NOT A CARE IN THE
WORLD:

YOUR BEST FRIEND'S WEDDING

YOUR BEST FRIEND IS GETTING HITCHED! YOU DIDN'T MAKE THE BRIDESMAID LIST, SO YOU NEED TO MAKE SURE YOU LOOK SHOWSTOPPING AS YOU'RE KINDA IN LOVE WITH THE BEST MAN... LET REPHRASE THAT, YOU'RE OBSESSED WITH HIM. PLAN YOUR LOOK ON THESE PAGES!

DRAW THE DRESS:

BRIDE... STEP ASIDE!

WHAT COLOURS ARE YOU USING FOR YOUR MAKE-UP?

DRAW THE EARRINGS:

PROS AND CONS OF
WEARING A FASCINATOR:

PRO   **CON**

- I CAN HIDE
FOOD AND
SPLIT ENDS
UNDER IT.

USING SHAPES AND
COLOURS, HOW DID YOU
FEEL WHEN YOU DIDN'T
CATCH THE BOUQUET BUT
MAUREEN DID?

DRAW THE HAIRSTYLE YOU CHOSE FOR THE
BIG DAY:

THE JOB INTERVIEW

YOU'VE GOT A BIG INTERVIEW TODAY. YOU DON'T REALLY KNOW WHAT THE JOB IS BUT IT PAYS GOOD MONEY AND GIVES YOU CHANCE TO WEAR THAT NEW PENCIL SKIRT. TAKE A DEEP BREATH AND GO GET 'EM TIGER.

DRAW A CLASSY UP-DO:

DRAW THE REST OF YOUR OUTFIT AROUND THIS PENCIL SKIRT:

LIST YOUR TOP 3 CAREER GOALS:

1

2

3 OWN A UNICORN PETTING ZOO...

USING SHAPES AND COLOUR, DRAW THE SEXUAL TENSION BETWEEN YOU AND THE INTERVIEWER:

WHATEVER YOU DO, <u>DON'T</u> WEAR THOSE COURT SHOES YOUR MOTHER BOUGHT YOU, DEFACE THESE:

WHOA. THAT WAS LIKE SUPER HOT...

HOW GOOD DOES YOUR BUM LOOK IN YOUR OUTFIT?

THE FIRST DATE

IT'S FRIDAY NIGHT AND YOU'VE BEEN ASKED ON A DATE, A PERFECT TIME TO SHOW OFF YOUR NEW STYLE! NOW, YOU WANT TO BLOW THEM AWAY WITH YOUR STYLE CRED AND THE BEST WAY TO DO THIS IS WITH AN S. O. R. (SECOND. OUTFIT. REVEAL.). IT'S ALL ABOUT GETTING THE STATEMENT JACKET RIGHT, THEN WHEN YOU'RE ABOUT TO BE SEATED, BOOM! WHIP THAT JACKET OFF TO REVEAL YOUR KILLER OUTFIT UNDERNEATH!

OUTFIT WITH AMAZING, STYLED-UP JACKET (THINK A MAC, BLAZER OR LEATHER)

...THEN TAKE IT OFF TO REVEAL YOUR JAW-DROPPING OUTFIT UNDERNEATH:

DRAW YOUR HAIR
FOR TONIGHT:

MAKE A LIST OF FIRST DATE DO'S
AND DON'TS PLEASE...

DOs!

- FLIRT LIKE
  IT'S YOUR CAREER.

DON'Ts!

- EAT SPAGHETTI
  IN PUBLIC. EVER.
  EVEN THE WAITER
  WAS TRAUMATISED.

DRAW YOUR DATE:

WHAT DID THEY SAY ABOUT YOUR
OUTFIT?!

ACCESSORIES

YES, THIS IS WHERE WE TALK ABOUT SHOES. AND BAGS, AND BELTS, AND HATS. I LOVE HATS!

FILL IN EACH ITEM WITH HOW MANY YOU OWN, FOLLOWED BY HOW MANY YOU ACTUALLY WEAR. C'MON NOW, BE HONEST.

SHOES — OWN ☐ WEAR ☐

HATS — OWN ☐ WEAR ☐

BELTS — OWN ☐ WEAR ☐

SCARVES — OWN ☐ WEAR ☐

BAGS — OWN ☐ WEAR ☐

STRIPPER SHOES — OWN ☐ WEAR ☐

LET'S GET THIS OUT OF THE WAY, DRAW OR LIST ALL THE SHOES YOU OWN:

OI! YOU FORGOT THE PAIR YOU
BOUGHT ON YOUR LUNCH BREAK
LAST WEEK...

HAT TIP

THINK YOU DON'T SUIT HATS? THINK AGAIN. WITHOUT LOOKING IN THE MIRROR (I KNOW, WITH YOUR ASTOUNDING BEAUTY IT'S HARD ISN'T IT?) PLACE A HAT ON YOUR HEAD, ADJUST TO HOW YOU THINK IT SHOULD BE PLACED. THEN LOOK IN THE MIRROR AND VOILA! YOUR HEAD IS HAT-READY BABY. TRUST ME, THIS WORKS.

ADD TO AND DECORATE LADY MARY'S FANCY HAT:

ADD COLOUR AND PRINT TO THESE SEXY HATS:

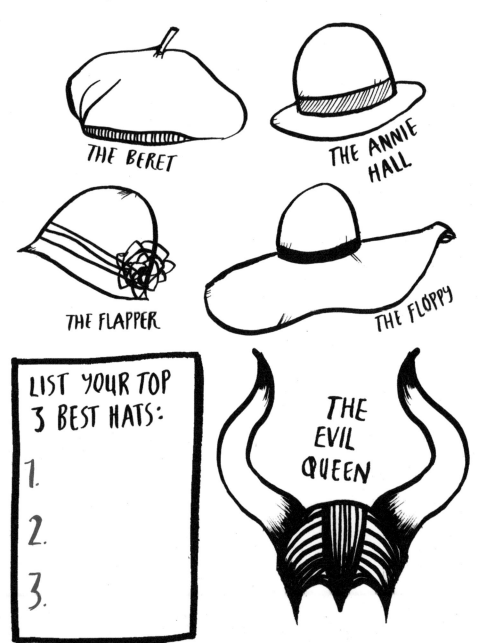

THE BERET

THE ANNIE HALL

THE FLAPPER

THE FLOPPY

LIST YOUR TOP 3 BEST HATS:

1.

2.

3.

THE EVIL QUEEN

LUPITA NYONG'O
(MARCH 7st, 1983 – PRESENT)

LUPITA IS A FILM AND MUSIC VIDEO DIRECTOR, WRITER AND OSCAR-WINNING ACTRESS. SHE IS THE FIRST KENYAN ACTRESS TO WIN AN OSCAR AND THE SIXTH BLACK ACTRESS TO WIN THE AWARD. SHE IS A CONSTANT RED CARPET WINNER, EXPERIMENTING WITH NEW STYLES AND LOTS OF COLOUR. SHE IS ALSO VERY AWESOME.

AND SO I HOPE THAT MY PRESENCE ON YOUR SCREENS AND IN MAGAZINES MAY LEAD YOU, YOUNG GIRL, ON A SIMILAR JOURNEY. THAT YOU WILL FEEL THE VALIDATION FOR YOUR BEAUTY, BEAUTY BUT ALSO GET TO THE DEEPER BUSINESS OF FEELING BEAUTIFUL INSIDE.

GIVE A GIRL THE RIGHT TIGHTS, SHE CAN RULE THE WORLD. ON THESE PAGES DESIGN SOME PRINTS AND PATTERNS ON THESE DIFFERENT BODY SHAPES! I WANT TO SEE A PRINT EXTRAVAGANZA THAT WOULD MAKE HENRY HOLLAND QUIVER IN HIS BROGUES.

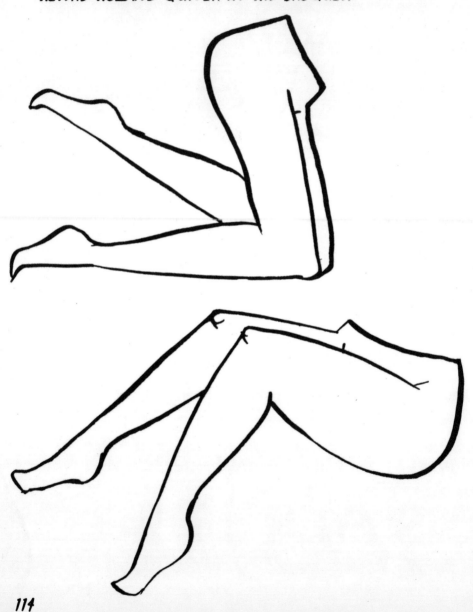

GEEK OUT

DRAW YOUR FACE UNDER THESE GEEK GLASSES.
LET ME SEE YOUR BEST HIPSTER FACE.

DRAW YOUR DREAM HANDBAG:

WEAR YOUR HAIR

FLICK IT, TIE IT, TOP-KNOT IT. EVERYTHING YOU SHOULD KNOW ABOUT YOUR BEST ACCESSORY.

DRAW YOUR FACE UNDER ALL THESE DOs:

THE POB

THE TALK SHOW HOST

**THE FEMALE
CHUCK NORRIS**

THE FOXY BROWN

HOW TO DO A TOP KNOT

CAN'T BE BOTHERED WITH SPLIT ENDS TODAY? THEN LET'S DO A TOP KNOT, BABY.

1 BRUSH YOUR HAIR BACK INTO A PONYTAIL. YOU CAN USE YOUR FINGERS TO COMB THROUGH AS FACE IT, YOU'RE LAZY.

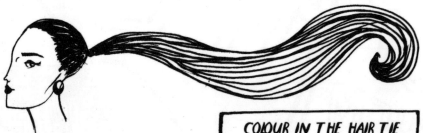

2 TWIST THAT TAIL RIGHT UP ONTO THAT HEAD OF YOURS. HAVE A HAIR TIE ON STANDBY...

COLOUR IN THE HAIR TIE

3 HOLD THE KNOT, THEN PULL THE REST OF YOUR HAIR OVER IT. TIE IN WITH THE HAIR TIE I MADE YOU COLOUR IN.

DRAW YOUR TOP KNOT:

I ♥ VOLUME

4 HAIRSPRAY IS MY SECOND FAVOURITE THING IN THE UNIVERSE. AFTER DINOSAURS OF COURSE. GET SOME SPRAY TO HOLD YOUR KNOT IN AND PRESTO, YOU'VE GOT HIGH-FASHION HAIR NAILED!

TRY OUT YOUR FACE UNDER THESE TOP KNOTS:

SECOND DATE DO

YOU'VE GOT THAT IMPORTANT DINNER DATE WITH RICHARD THE HAIR MODEL. YOU NEED TO UP THE STAKES HAIR-WISE AS HIS HAIR HAS WAY MORE BOUNCE THAN YOURS. AS YOU'RE SAT DOWN FOR A FEW HOURS, MAKE TONIGHT'S ENSEMBLE ALL ABOUT THE HAIR! MAKE ME PROUD.

DRAW OR LIST ALL THE HAIR ACCESSORIES IN YOUR AMAZING HAIR TONIGHT:

COLOUR THOSE LUSCIOUS LIPS!

WRITE DOWN 3 AMAZING THINGS ABOUT YOUR HAIR:

1.

2.

3.

DRAW HOW YOU THINK YOU AND
YOUR HAIR LOOK TO RICHARD ON
THE DINNER DATE.

HAIROGRAPHY

A KILLER HAIR FLICK CAN GET YOU THROUGH MANY SOCIAL SITUATIONS. NOT ON THE GUEST LIST FOR THAT NEW BAR? BREAK OUT YOUR BEST SIDE-SWISH AND YOU'RE IN. GO AND STICK ON SOME QUEEN BEY AND LET YOUR HAIR DOWN. DRAW THE HAIR ON THESE HAIR MODELS!

1. THE SIDE-SWISH

PICK A SHOULDER, PUT YOUR HAIR ON IT AND FLICK FROM THE OTHER SHOULDER. PERFECT FOR 'WTF' MOMENTS IN LIFE.

2. THE DOUBLE-TAP

IS SOMEONE GIVING YOU RAGE TODAY? THEN PUT YOUR HAIR ON BOTH YOUR SHOULDERS, FLICK ONE SIDE OFF AND THEN THE OTHER. FINISH OFF WITH A SHOULDER AND AN ARCHED EYEBROW.

3. THE SLOW-MO

YOU'RE IN THE LIBRARY, YOU SEE THAT GUY YOU STALK AT THE SUPERMARKET. TURN, SLOWLY FLICK YOUR HAIR AND FLASH A SWEET SMILE. MAYBE EVEN THROW IN A GIGGLE. YOUR EYES MEET, HE TURNS AND... WALKS OUT. OH SHIT.

4. THE SEDUCTION SWISH

THIS IS THE JACKPOT OF HAIROGRAPHY. IF YOU CAN NAIL THIS, YOU CAN ACHIEVE ANYTHING. TO BE USED WHEN TRYING TO SEDUCE OR WHEN BEYOND RAGE, PUT BOTH HANDS ON THE TABLE, HEAD DOWN AND FLICK RIGHT UP! ACCENTUATE THAT JAWLINE AND DO A FACE A PORN STAR WOULD BE ENVIOUS OF!

GO CRAZY. DRAW ME THE BEST SEDUCTION SWISH. EVER:

REMEMBER...

BIG HAIR DON'T CARE!

HOW TO BE FIERCE!

CHANNEL YOUR INNER GAGA, LEARN HOW TO SIDEYE AND MEET PENNY, THE VINTAGE-HIPSTER MERMAID...

WHEN IN DOUBT OF CERTAIN SOCIAL SITUATIONS, ALWAYS MAKE SURE YOU CHANNEL YOUR INNER DIVA! MINE'S A BIT OF LADY GAGA. WHO IS YOURS?

CHANNEL MY INNER

BACKING DANCERS →

HOW TO SIDE-EYE

THE GUY AT WORK SAYS HE LOVES YOUR NEW LOOK AND THAT YOU LOOK 'FUNKY'. HOWEVER, PRUNELLA WHO SITS ACROSS FROM YOU DISAGREES BY THROWING YOU A FILTHY LOOK. POSITION PRUNELLA'S FACE NEAR TO YOURS, ARCH AN EYEBROW AND SIDE-EYE HER INTO NEXT WEEK!

DAMN SHE'S GOT GOOD HAIR. COLOUR IT IN

PRUNELLA VAN
THUNDERPUMP

SISTERHOOD

YOU AND YOUR FRIENDS HAVE
STYLED YOURSELVES UP A HELL
OF A LOT RECENTLY AND LOOK
DAMN FINE! STICK A PHOTO
IN ON THE OPPOSITE PAGE,
RIP THE PAGE OUT AND FRAME
IT! AND YES, THOSE ARE UNICATS...
CATS THAT ARE ALSO UNICORNS.

NOW TAKE A PIC AND TAG IT ON INSTAGRAM WITH #MAPMYSTYLE!

BANG ON TREND

SO NOW YOU'VE BEEN ON THIS FASHION ADVENTURE WITH ME, I WANT THE NEW YOU TO FILL IN THESE BOXES WITH WHAT YOU'VE LEARNT:

USING SHAPES AND COLOUR, DRAW HOW YOU FEEL WHEN YOU LOOK AT THE NEW YOU IN THE MIRROR:

WHAT ARE YOUR WARDROBE STAPLES?

HOW MUCH WAS YOUR LAST CREDIT CARD BILL?

(DON'T BLAME ME)

DRAW OR LIST WHO INSPIRES YOUR STYLE:

DON'T. FORGET. ME!

USING SHAPES AND COLOUR, SHOW ME WHAT 'I'M HAPPY BEING ME AND I'M FREAKING AMAZING' LOOKS LIKE:

WHERE DO YOU SEE YOURSELF IN 5 YEARS' TIME? SHOW ME:

MARILYN MONROE

(JUNE 1st 1926 - AUGUST 5TH 1962)

NORMA JEAN MORTENSON WAS A HUGE SEX SYMBOL DURING THE 1950s AND EARLY 60s. SHE WAS AN ACTRESS, SINGER AND MODEL. HER HOURGLASS FIGURE AND ABILITY TO LOOK SMOULDERING OVER AN AIR VENT WAS THE TALK OF TINSELTOWN.

GO FIND A BOOK, SONG, FILM, BLOG, SOUND, PERSON, POEM, ANYTHING THAT YOU FEEL INSPIRES YOU AND YOUR STYLE. THEN, COME TO THIS PAGE AND WRITE DOWN WHAT IT WAS BELOW

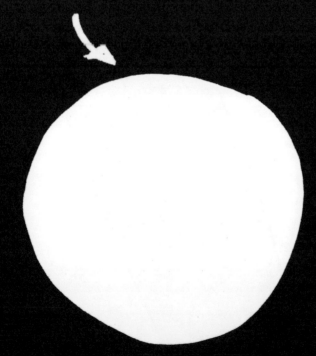

BE WHOEVER YOU WANT TO BE...
JUST LIKE PENNY, THE HIPSTER
VINTAGE MERMAID HERE. COLOUR HER
IN AND ADD SOME AQUATIC FRIENDS
FOR HER TO TALK TO ABOUT SEASHELLS
AND STUFF:

...IS AWESOME

STICK IN/DRAW A PICTURE OF ONE PERSON WHO HAS INSPIRED YOU IN LIFE. GO ON, GET AS SOPPY AS YOU LIKE...

NOW TAKE A PIC AND TAG IT ON INSTAGRAM WITH #MAPMYSTYLE!

FIN

THANK YOU

THANK YOU TO THE GREAT FOLKS AT HUCK & PUCKER, MY BUDDIES IN BRIGHTON, LDN, MANCHESTER AND NARNIA (YOU KNOW WHO YOU ARE) FOR BEING THERE. FINALLY, TO MY MUM, DAD AND SISTER FOR PUTTING UP WITH MY BAD SHIRTS, DIVA STROPS AND BIG HAIR. I PROMISE ONE DAY, I'LL BUY YOU A NEW HOOVER. IF NOT A HOOVER, THEN MAYBE A TEAPOT?

IF YOU'RE INTERESTED IN FINDING OUT MORE ABOUT OUR PRODUCTS, FIND US ON FACEBOOK AT HUCK AND PUCKER AND FOLLOW US ON TWITTER @HUCKANDPUCKER.

WWW.HUCKANDPUCKER.COM